MODEL RAILROADING

by

Michael E. Goodman

CRESTWOOD HOUSE

New York

Maxwell Macmillan Canada
Toronto

Maxwell Macmillan International
New York   Oxford   Singapore   Sydney

Library of Congress Cataloging-in-Publication Data
Goodman, Michael E.
 Model Railroading / by Michael E. Goodman. — 1st ed.
  p. cm. — (Hobby guides)
 Includes index.
 Summary: An introduction to model railroading with information on the different types of models, the building of scenery, and the clubs concerning this hobby.
 ISBN 0-89686-620-3
 1. Railroads—Models—Juvenile literature. [1. Railroads—Models. 2. Models and modelmaking.]
I. Title. II. Series.
TF197.G63 1993
625.1'9—dc20
                           91-15853

Photo Credits
All photos courtesy of *Model Railroader* magazine

Macmillan Publishing Company
866 Third Avenue
New York, NY 10022

Maxwell Macmillan Canada, Inc.
1200 Eglinton Avenue East
Suite 200
Don Mills, Ontario M3C 3N1

CRESTWOOD HOUSE

Macmillan Publishing Company is part of the Maxwell Communication Group of Companies.

Produced by Flying Fish Studio

Printed in the United States of America

First edition

10 9 8 7 6 5 4 3 2 1

CONTENTS

The Exciting World of Model Railroading 5

What Is Model Railroading? 10

Choosing Your First Model Railroading Set 14

Setting Up Your First Train Set 22

Planning a Model Railroad Layout 25

Adding Realism to Your Layout 31

Weathering Your Model Railroad 34

Modular Model Railroading 36

A Model Railroading Club....................38

For More Information 41

Glossary 45

Index 48

Creating your own miniature train line can be quite an adventure.

THE EXCITING WORLD OF MODEL RAILROADING

If you are thinking about a fast, powerful way to get somewhere today, you probably have in mind a supersonic jet plane streaking across the sky or a sleek automobile or truck racing along a superhighway. But not too many years ago, your first thought would have been of a train with its locomotive belching steam and smoke and its lonely whistle wailing into the night. Trains were once the fastest and most exciting way to travel across the country.

Many people still get a special feeling when they ride on a train or even see one passing. A famous British novelist named E. M. Forster once wrote that a railroad station is "our gate to the glorious and the unknown." He meant that starting a train ride is like beginning a great adventure of sight and sound. But if, like most people, you don't often get an opportunity to travel on a full-size train, you can still take part in the adventure by creating your own miniature train line and directing your own model trains along it.

Nearly half a million Americans re-create the excitement of real-life trains by building and operating model railroad setups in their own homes. Some people put together a simple circular pattern of track and send a store-bought train set around it. Others may devise intricate layouts with cars and scenery they have built themselves to capture closely the look and feel of a real train and the entire environment in which it might run.

Many historians believe that the modern industrial age began when the first trains started traveling through Europe and the United States in the 1830s. Suddenly it became possible to go from place to place or to transport goods quickly and efficiently. The first railroads were also the testing grounds for many important inventions, such as steam engines and rail designs and switches. The biggest challenges were often how to lay the steel tracks and get trains through to hard-to-reach places. The railroad builders might have to blast out and support a tunnel through a mountain of solid rock. Or they might have to devise a narrow **gauge** of rail to run along a treacherous mountainside or through a mountain pass to reach a gold or silver mine.

Not long after those first trains appeared, some engineers began building miniature ones. These trains were not toys. Instead, they were used as models to try out ideas for the real thing. Since they were doing real work, these early models were built with painstaking detail. Then toymakers got into the act as early as the 1850s. The early toy trains were primarily made out of tin and were propelled by a

Many modelers enjoy building structures, cars and locomotives from scratch. This scene was built with scale stripwood.

clockwork (or wound spring) mechanism. Later model trains were made of cast iron and were pulled by a string instead of running on rails. By the late 1800s, model trains became popular playthings and collectibles.

Trains may not be as important today as they once were for transportation, but model railroading is more widespread than ever before. A quick visit to any hobby store will prove this point. You'll find dozens of simple or elaborate train sets. There will be hundreds of examples of locomotives with passenger or freight cars. Some of these will be already constructed while some will be build-it-yourself kits. You will find a whole world of accessories to help make your railroad layout seem real. You'll also find a variety of magazines and books to help you get started on, or learn more about, model railroading.

Model railroads encourage hobbyists to use their imaginations. They ask hobbyists to try out their own techniques for constructing exciting, real-life train layouts or for creating a whole miniature environment as part of their model setups.

There is something for everyone in the exciting world of model railroading. This book will help you learn more about how to begin the hobby and how to improve on different techniques for planning, laying out, and running a model railroad. It will also provide you with sources for additional information about toy trains and model railroading. So climb aboard and begin your own adventure to the "glorious and unknown."

(photo left): Layouts come in all shapes and sizes. This model train builder created a layout within a glass coffee table.

WHAT IS MODEL RAILROADING?

Model railroading is more than just hooking up a train set and watching it run around a circular track layout. It's true that most people get started on the hobby that way, but model railroading isn't something you do by simply watching. Like all good hobbies, it involves taking part in the action. Your activities may include reading catalogs or magazines, drawing blueprints, building cars or scenery, wiring the track and some accessories, painting, **weathering** (making cars or scenery look weather-beaten), or merely collecting and displaying. You'll need to apply your knowledge of history, electronics, mathematics, art, and several other subjects—in a special, fun way.

You don't need a lot of space or a lot of money to be a model railroader, but you do need patience and imagination. Some model railroaders get totally involved in their hobby. One man in Wisconsin spent more than 400 hours constructing a **trestle** from over 4,000 individual wooden pieces that he designed and cut out himself. His trestle is an exact replica of one he remembers from his childhood. So is his entire train setup. It fills the whole basement of his house.

Other model train builders really let their imaginations run wild. A French modeler built an entire setup on a 1:1000 scale, with a locomotive only $5/16$ of an inch long. He can run his set easily around the brim of a hat.

And other model train owners just can't get enough. A British railroader kept his coal-fired steam locomotive going for more than 27 hours, in which time it covered a world record distance of more than 144 miles without stopping. Another British team of railroaders guided their model train consisting of an engine and 6 coaches on a nonstop trip of 678 miles over a period of 36 days.

Most model railroaders are not out to set records. They get involved in the hobby to have fun and to create something unique.

There are two types of serious railroad hobbyists. One type is a **collector** and the other is a **modeler**.

A collector enjoys finding and owning replicas of famous model trains and displaying them. Like collectors of stamps, coins, comic books, or baseball cards—model railroad collectors want to make sure that the pieces of their collection are authentic and kept in a way that maintains their beauty and value. Collectors often specialize in trains of a particular time period or of a particular style. They often keep their prize locomotives, cars, or accessories in the original boxes. Sometimes they display them on shelves or in special cases.

Some model trains may be very valuable. One train set built in Germany near the turn of the century sold at an auction a few years ago for more than $35,000. And if your grandfather, as a boy in the 1930s, happened to buy a "Mickey and Minnie Mouse" handcar for $1, his toy could now be worth as much as $900!

For most model railroaders, the joy of the hobby is not in simply owning valuable locomotives or cars, but in putting them to work. That often means not only buying or building a train set, laying track, and wiring the setup, but

The Burlington Zephyr *was the first streamlined passenger diesel in the United States. It made its debut in 1934. This model of the train was built with plastic passenger cars and plastic sheet material.*

also designing and creating an entire world in which the train can run. This type of hobbyist is called a modeler.

Modelers come in all ages, shapes, and sizes. And most have individual purposes and goals for their hobby. Some like the challenge of building miniature things. They construct their own locomotives and cars from kits or from scratch and may even create their own track. Others start with a boxed train set and track pieces and then add on to them in order to create something unique and personal. Some modelers are very concerned that every piece of their setups be in perfect **scale**—even trees and mountain passes. Others focus primarily on re-creating a train line they have ridden on themselves or read about in books or magazines. One thing that all modelers have in common is a love for trains and what they represent.

No matter how you begin, one fact is clear: You'll never find yourself alone once you become a model railroader. There are more than 250,000 serious model railroaders in the United States alone and lots more throughout the world. You can share your knowledge and questions with other model railroaders in your town or all around the globe through clubs, magazines, books, or letters.

But first, you have to get started....

CHOOSING YOUR FIRST MODEL RAILROADING SET

You have already read about some of the reasons to begin model railroading. However, before you spend any money on this serious hobby, start by doing some research. Here are a few steps you might take at the beginning:

• Visit a hobby shop and get an idea of all the equipment that is available there. Compare the different setups and accessories. See how much they cost or how difficult they are to construct. A hobby store is a better place to start than a department store. You'll find experts in a hobby store to answer your questions and help you make the best choices. You'll also find the largest selection of trains to choose from. And you're sure to find other model railroaders there to engage in a conversation. Most hobbyists love to talk about their creations almost as much as work on them.

• Visit experienced model railroaders and observe their creations. Talk with them about how they got started on the hobby and why they enjoy it.

• Read some of the magazines devoted to the hobby. Most of them are available at hobby shops.

• Decide how much room you have available to devote to your train setup. Determine if this space can be dedicated to your hobby. Perhaps it has to be shared for such activities as sleeping, studying, storing things, eating, and so on. You might need to make your setup portable if you have to share the space.

• Find out if there is a model railroading club nearby. The hobby shop owner can be a good source of information.

• Think about how handy you are with tools, electric wiring, and various raw materials.

• Think about how important historical authenticity, scale and gauge, and a realistic total setting are to you.

• Think about your own tastes in trains. Are you more interested in passenger trains or freight trains? Do you want your train setup to include a town setting, a mountain pass, a tunnel, a yard or siding—or all of the above? Do you want your setup to have a particular look and feel?

• Decide how much money and time you can devote to the hobby. These two considerations are important ones. They will help you decide how complex you can make your layout. They will also give you ideas about how much of your setup can be store-bought and how much you should build yourself.

This is the Kitty Hawk Central, *a simple layout designed for easy construction by beginners.*

Once you have done your initial research, you're ready to proceed to the next step—deciding which train set is right for you. There are lots of choices.

One of the prime considerations should be the size of your setup. Size is usually measured in scale and gauge. Scale means the proportion of your miniaturized model to the full-size original train. For example, 1 inch in your model could represent 48, 87, 160, or some other full-size measurement in inches. Gauge is the width of your train's track. It is measured from the inside of one rail to the inside of the other. The exact width of the track you use will depend on the scale you are using and the original train setup you are modeling.

There are 17 different scales listed by the **National Model Railroad Association (NMRA)**. However, only 6 are easy to obtain, and 3 of these are utilized by nearly all modelers—HO, N, and O scales.

Nearly three-quarters of all model railroaders choose **HO scale**, in which 1 inch on the model represents 87 inches on the original. What makes it so popular? The size is small enough to allow room for a complete layout that has good curves. These curves are broad enough to permit smooth movement of models of even modern 80-foot passenger and freight cars along the track. It is also large enough to allow you to see and re-create exact details of the original train cars even on your tiny models.

An HO layout with lots of interesting variations and scenery can comfortably be set up on a 4 x 8 foot plywood sheet. Of course, with more space, you can incorporate even more track options and setting details into your layout.

The water in this N scale layout may look deep, but it's actually just $^1/_8$ inch thick.

Suppose you don't have enough space for a 4 x 8 foot setup. Then you might choose the second most popular train scale—N. **N scale** is approximately half the size of HO, or about 1 inch representing 160 inches. Most N-scale equipment is in the ready to run category because the tiny size makes it very difficult to construct authentic-looking locomotives or rolling stock on your own. One advantage of N scale over HO scale is that you can set up and view more train cars and scenery in a small space. You could probably set up a realistic N-scale layout on a space as small as 2 x 4 feet.

If you have more room or just like larger models to work with or run, you might choose **O scale** for your setup. O scale is approximately twice the size of HO (in fact, HO stands for "half O"), with 1 inch representing 48 inches. You would probably need at least an 8 x 16 foot space to construct a workable O-scale train layout. One advantage of O scale is that it is easier to see and create intricate details on the larger models.

There are other scales to choose from, but HO, N, and O are the most popular and easiest sizes for which to obtain parts.

The track on which your model train rides should also be proportional to that used by the original train you are modeling. There are two major types of track width—**standard gauge** and **narrow gauge**.

Long ago, the U.S. Congress established the standard width for real railroad track at 56 $\frac{1}{2}$ inches. If you are using an HO scale model train, standard gauge track for your model would be .65 of an inch wide ($\frac{1}{87}$ of $56\frac{1}{2}$ inches).

However, not all train tracks (or the wheels of the cars) were laid out in standard gauge, particularly in mountainous areas where narrower tracks and a smaller wheel base were needed to permit trains to negotiate tight curves. Some tracks were laid out as close together as 3 or even 2 feet. These types of trains were called "narrow gauge." You might want to create your own narrow gauge model train, particularly if your space is limited. However, there is less ready to run equipment available in narrow gauge, so you may end up having to construct much of your rolling stock from kits or from scratch.

This is an example of a nicely detailed HO scale scene.

The scale and gauge you choose for your first model railroading set are important technical considerations. But there are other important things to think about as well. For example, think about which historical period interests you the most or which type or model of train is the one you would like to spend time creating or operating. After all, you're the person in charge of this railroad!

Here are a few facts you might want to consider in choosing your first train. There are three basic types of locomotives: Steam, diesel, and electric. And these locomotives come in many different sizes and shapes. You need to decide which one looks best to you and which fits your vision of *your* railroad.

There are also four basic categories of **rolling stock**: Freight cars, passenger cars, cabooses, and maintenance equipment. That's just the beginning. There are at least ten different kinds of freight cars—from boxcars to log cars to circus cars. In the passenger-car category are coaches, Pullman cars, diners, baggage cars, and automobile carriers. Maintenance equipment includes cranes, derricks, and snowplows, to name just a few.

You can also choose historic or modern equipment for your railroad. One of the advantages to old-time train cars is that they were shorter than modern-day ones, so you can run them on less track and build in tighter curves. But a modern train line may be your choice because of the innovations these cars display.

Most locomotives and rolling stock can be purchased in sets or individually. Or you can build your own from kits or

This 4 x 8 foot HO scale layout is set in a scene from the southwest United States.

from scratch. The choices are almost endless. It all depends on your taste and budget. So head to a hobby store and begin exploring and asking questions.

SETTING UP YOUR FIRST TRAIN SET

Once you have decided to become a model railroader and have chosen your first train set, it is time to really get started. This chapter will provide you with some good advice for assuring that your first train will run smoothly and safely.

Start by locating the instructions inside the train set box. Some sets contain very good instructions, while others come with only basic information. In any case, read the instructions carefully. Then assemble the pieces—the cars and track—step-by-step. Take your time. Also keep all of the different boxes for safe storage or in case you need to return a defective part to the store. (Collectors also give added value to cars stored in their original boxes.)

You will need a few basic tools to help you put the set together. A screwdriver with a narrow blade is a must for attaching wires to the track and the **power pack** terminals. You might also find a pair of needle-nose pliers to be helpful for different tasks. Other handy tools include a hobby knife, files, sandpaper, cotton-tipped swabs, and a scale ruler.

Another good piece of advice is to avoid oiling the engine or the wheels before you get started. The moving parts of your set should operate smoothly without any extra grease. Besides, any excess oil could mix with dust to form deposits on the wheels or track. This could hinder the electrical contact needed to make your train run properly.

Dust may also become a problem if you choose to set your train up directly on a floor or carpet. Instead, plan to construct your layout on a piece of plywood large enough to hold the track and allow for enlarging the original layout or adding pieces of scenery.

When you put the pieces of track together, be careful not to bend the **rail joiners**—the little metal connectors that link the pieces of track. You might buy a few spares at the hobby shop, just to be on the safe side. Make sure the track pieces fit together comfortably with the joiners; don't force them. There should be as little gap as possible between rail joiners—no more than the thickness of one piece of paper. Once the track is together, run your finger across the joints to feel for roughness or different heights. Sometimes, you may accidentally have connected a joiner to the bottom of a rail rather than the center. The result could be misalignment that might lead to derailments when you run your train across the track.

Next, connect the wires to the terminals of the power pack before you plug in the power pack to a wall outlet. The power pack uses low voltage and low current, so it shouldn't provide any painful shocks, but it is best to play it safe. If your power pack contains both **alternating (AC)** and **direct current (DC)** terminals, make sure that you hook up the track to the DC terminals. The AC output of most train transformers will ruin the motor of your locomotive. The AC terminals are for accessories, such as remote switching machines, lights, or movable crossing gates.

Overhead electric wires and streetcars can give a realistic look to your model.

The power pack that comes with your set is probably only large enough to handle the track and engine included in the set itself. If you plan to run several engines with your set to pull additional cars, or you want to run several trains independent of each other, you may need to purchase a larger power pack or additional packs.

All of this may seem like a lot of work, but, after all, you plan on running your train set for a long, long time. And doing things right at the start will make this possible.

PLANNING A MODEL
RAILROAD LAYOUT

Most model railroaders are not content just to put together a packaged train set and run it on the round or oval track layout provided with the set. Instead, they want to transform their "toy" train into a "model" of a real railroad operating on a realistic stretch of track in a realistic environment. The expanded layout doesn't have to be very complicated, and the scenery doesn't have to be totally accurate. It just has to satisfy your own mental picture of something unique.

Lots of materials are available to help you expand your train set into something more creative—from track, to additional locomotives and rolling stock, to large power packs, to bridges and trestles, to scenery elements. Most of these items can be bought at hobby stores, fully constructed or in build-it-yourself kits. You can also create much of the scenery or even pieces of track yourself, if you're creative and handy with tools. You'll learn more about this in the next chapter.

Start with your imagination and paper. Make a rough sketch of your track layout. Then transform that sketch into a full-size scale drawing. Some hobby shops have track templates that will help you accurately draw curves and switches to scale. You might add mountains, tunnels, bodies of water, buildings, or bridges into your drawing to make sure that they fit with your plan and your available space. Your track plan may need to be changed somewhat to accommodate the scenery you envision. You may also discover that you can't have everything you want, but don't let that stop you.

The central element of your layout is the track for your railroad. You can purchase additional pieces of track in the proper scale to match the track included in a basic train set in a variety of shapes—straight pieces, left- or right-hand curves, two-way pieces that come with remote-control switches, or flexible track you can manipulate to meet your needs. Before you purchase any new track, however, think about how much space you have available, what shape you want your layout to have, how large a train you want to run on the track, and how much power you will need to run the train along the track.

Detailed and scenic layouts do not have to be large. This N scale layout is just 2 x 4 feet.

Your track can take any shape. Several possible track plans that you might follow are mentioned below. However, if you're just starting out, you might want to begin with a track plan that you can find already described in a book or magazine. It should be possible to re-create this plan with the proper materials outlined in the publication. Someone at your local hobby shop will be happy to help you find a good beginning layout.

If you do decide to design your own layout configuration, ask yourself some of the following questions:

How much space do I have and what is the shape of that space?

The space may limit your design somewhat. Keep in mind, for example, that curves must be gradual to avoid derailments. Because of this, they will require extra width in your layout. You also need to leave space around the table so that you can reach all parts of the track comfortably when you lay out the track or operate your train on it. You might also want to leave enough room for spectators. After all, you're going to want to show off your railroad.

*How many **switches**, crossings, or **turnouts** do I want?*

You will need to purchase the right track pieces to enable you to create these designs.

How much money will I need to spend on track, cars, and scenery?

Prepare a budget to help you decide how best to spend your money. Remember that you don't have to do everything at once, however. Your railroad can grow over time. Start with your basic needs.

How long will my turns need to be and will I need to bank the turns to make sure my train doesn't derail?

Your answers to these questions will once again depend on space and may affect what materials you need to buy or create.

Is part of my track going to be elevated?

If so, keep in mind that most model locomotives will not be able to pull a series of 4-5 cars over a grade of higher than 6 percent, so a rise of 6 inches will require at least 100 inches of track to accomplish.

Once your layout is developed and sketched, you are ready to begin building. Consider using one or more pieces of plywood as your base. These must be at least $1/2$-inch thick. Make sure the base is strong enough so it doesn't sag or warp. The base may be one large rectangle or several rectangles joined together to form a U, L, or S shape. Put your plywood onto a tabletop or attach it to sawhorses or legs you construct yourself. The base should be at least 40-48 inches above the ground so that you can work on it comfortably. You should also have a clearance of at least 36 inches above the base to permit room for scenery and for viewing once the layout is complete.

Then sketch the track plan with a pencil onto the plywood to serve as a guide when you lay the track.

Because real railroads run on a roadbed raised above the ground, most modelers also create their own roadbeds by using ready-made strips or by using materials such as cork, wood, or homosote, a wallboard type of material available from lumber yards. Arrange or cut out your roadbed materials so that they follow your track plan. Then tack them down with nails or staples.

Now you are finally ready to lay the track on top of the roadbed. Thin wire nails are best for this job. Make sure that the undersides of the nail heads barely touch the tops of the rail ties. If you pound them in too far, you may distort the ties and cause possible derailments. Make sure all rail joints are in line, and sight down the track frequently at eye level to detect any kinks. When you have all the track in place, run your fingertip along each joint and smooth any mismatches with a small file.

Your next problem is going to be wiring your layout. This doesn't need to be a complicated task, and you don't have to be an electrician to accomplish it. There are guidebooks available at hobby stores or libraries that deal with all aspects of model railroad wiring. You will also find clear instructions included with your power pack to help you handle any wiring needs. Follow the directions carefully rather than simply "winging" it.

Luckily, for most basic layouts, all you will have to do is hook up the wires from the power pack to the track. Then plug in the power pack and operate the controls. Make sure that you hook up the power wires for the locomotive to the DC terminals of the power pack. Attaching the wires to the AC terminals might burn out your locomotive. If your layout plan calls for a loop, however, you may have a potential problem to consider. Make sure that when the loop rejoins the main line that you haven't brought the positive side of the track in contact with the negative. That can lead to a short circuit.

Another consideration is to make sure that your power pack is strong enough to handle your needs. You can run two engines on one oval track at the same time and at the same speed with a single set of wires if the power pack is strong enough. The trains are going to start and stop at the same time in this case. If you want to run two trains independently of each other, however, you may need separate power packs, or a power pack with multiple controls, and a more complicated wiring scheme. Discuss your plans with the hobby store owner or an experienced model railroader.

One good tip is not to scrimp on the power pack(s) you buy to run your trains. Buy the best your budget will allow. Make sure the power pack(s) will be strong enough to meet your present and future needs.

ADDING REALISM
TO YOUR LAYOUT

Full-size trains run through a real environment. You may want to have your model trains wind through mountain passes, roar through tunnels, cross gorges, lakes or rivers, or race through Old West mining towns or modern cities. Ready-made scale models or build-it-yourself kits of a wide variety of environmental features—and even human figures—are available from hobby stores. You can purchase miniature trees, mountains, shrubs, buildings, or factories. The limits are only your imagination, your space, and your budget. Take another tour of the hobby shop to see what is available.

You can also build a lot of the scenic elements yourself. Realistic trees, for example, can be constructed using real ferns or twigs as a base. Then you can add bits of steel wool to form branches. You can spray the "tree" with paint and, while it is still wet, roll it in bits of green paper or foam rubber shreds. You can also create a tree by twisting a bundle of wires into branches and then attaching bits of green foam rubber or crepe paper to the wires. Bushes can be formed by shaping chunks of foam rubber, which are then painted. Walls and fences can be made from strips of balsa wood or pieces of metal tubing soldered together. Colored sawdust or pieces of felt can give the appearance of grass.

Mountains and tunnels can be a little more complicated. If you are building a mountain, first you need to define its shape. Study photographs to get some ideas. Then wad up old newspapers or paper towels around a support structure of wood or wire. Masking tape and water sprayed on the paper will help the mountain hold its shape. Next, dip strips of paper towels into a thin plaster solution to form the outer covering. A thickness of about $\frac{1}{4}$ inch is a good idea.

If you want to make a tunnel through the mountain, cut out a section of the plaster and remove enough paper from inside to allow the train track to pass through. You can create your own entrance and exit portals or buy them at the hobby store.

To give your mountain a rocky appearance, add more plaster and file it into craggy shapes or use liquid latex. You can also glue on mixtures of rock-like materials. To achieve the right color patterns, most modelers advise using only paint, not mixtures of gray, tan, rust, or white clothing dyes.

Carved plaster and plaster castings are two methods used to simulate rocks and mountains. A spray of india ink diluted in water with a few drops of detergent provides a good initial coloring for rockwork.

Bodies of water can be another problem. Real water is not a good idea, since water around electricity can be dangerous. You will want to use a material such as a clear resin, or liquid plastic. First, cut out or form a shallow bed for your body of water and shape the banks or shorelines. Then pour in the resin and let it harden. As it hardens, shape it the way you want it to look. You can even make ripples and drop in pieces of wood, rock, or vegetation. A body of water will require some type of bridge, of course, to allow your train to cross it. A variety of bridges are available ready-made or in kits. Or you can construct your own from different types of materials.

You can build embankments and rock walls with layers of polystyrene glued together, filed, and painted. Crumbled plaster and small stones can be added to give a rocky look. Pieces of moss or lichen can be attached to provide realistic-looking vegetation.

For town or city scenes, you can buy or create buildings and even paint backdrops—a sort of **diorama**.

All of the scenery for your layout doesn't have to be created at one time. Model railroading is meant to be a lifetime hobby. However, you will need to start with a basic idea of what some elements of the environment are going to be—bridges, rises in terrain, and tunnels, for example—to determine how much space your layout will require and what shape your track plan will take.

Take your time, be patient, and let your imagination run wild.

A miniaturized junkyard scene is given a sense of realism by the weathered old cars and parts lying about.

WEATHERING YOUR MODEL RAILROAD

Adding scenery is just one way to make your train setup seem more realistic. You can also apply chalk or paint to track, cars, or buildings to "age" your train set. These will look like layers of dirt and rust that have built up over time. This technique of aging your train is called weathering. You will need a piece of cotton, some fine sandpaper, a paintbrush, or a simple airbrush set up for the weathering process.

Before you begin weathering your train, study photographs of real trains to see how the cars look in real life. Or, if you live near a railroad, go visit and get a firsthand look. Notice where dirt or rust has built up. See how the colors have faded under sunlight and rain over time. That fading and aging is what you are going to try to re-create with paint or chalk. You will also notice that every car looks a little different, so you will want to weather each of your train cars in a slightly different way.

Your weathering colors don't have to be evenly distributed on any car. After all, you probably noticed in the photographs that dirt and rust don't build up evenly. Experiment and repaint, if you need to. And while you're spraying, you might even let some of your colors drop onto the tracks, rocks, or other scenic details to simulate the effect of smoke and dirt on them.

Weathering parts with a rust-colored spray or brush paint will give them an aged look.

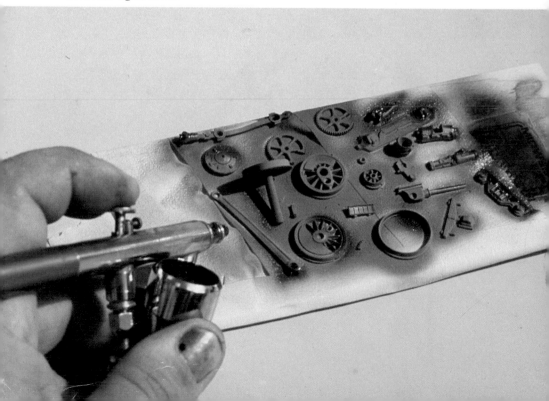

MODULAR MODEL RAILROADING

Two things that hold back some beginning model railroaders are time and space. In your mind, you picture a series of trains running through several different settings. However, you don't think you have the time or space to create that railroad. If that's the case, you might consider **modular model railroading**.

Modular model railroading involves creating an overall layout in several small segments, or modules. Each of the modules is large enough to incorporate plenty of scenery and track work all by itself. Then you can link the separate modules to form a complete railroad. For example, one module might consist of a rail yard and terminal, another of a small town with factories or other buildings, another of a piece of countryside or a mountain setting, and another of a separate branch line that connects to the main line.

A module can be a diorama in which you incorporate a scenery backdrop with a small area of track on which your train can stand or run. You can even fit a diorama on a bookshelf or dresser top. This type of setup is easy to work on and to move from place to place. As you become more talented at creating dioramas, you can find ways to link them to form a bigger layout. But you must plan for this growth from the beginning. Little by little, your separate modules can grow to take up an entire room or basement, as the amount of space you can devote to your model railroad increases.

Several model railroading clubs around the country are organized around the idea of modular layouts. Individual

Modular layouts allow modelers to build a small section of a layout on their own, then combine it with other modules.

members or groups create separate modules in N or HO scale, following an overall plan. The modules are then joined together to form an entire complex railroad for train shows. Often, the modules can be linked in a different order each time, with only the four "corner" modules staying the same so that a circular layout is possible anytime. You'll learn more about model railroading clubs in the next chapter of this book.

One of the great things about modular model railroading is that it will give you a chance to develop and improve your skills over a long period of time. You won't feel the pressure of creating a whole railroad at once. It will also give you an opportunity to work with others to create something bigger and more special than you might be able to accomplish all by yourself.

A MODEL RAILROADING CLUB

Earlier in this book, you read that you'll never be alone once you become a model railroader. You can find lots of other people with interests similar to yours who will be happy to share ideas and techniques with you.

One of the best ways to find other model railroaders is to join a model railroading club. Nearly every large city in the United States has a club devoted to model trains. The members meet regularly to discuss their hobby and their individual layouts. In many cases, club members work together to create a large or complex project, such as a modular system, as discussed in the previous chapter. They may also sponsor train shows, demonstrations, or auctions.

Joining a club is also a way to let you specialize in what you like best—such as wiring, laying track, or weathering cars. But you probably won't want to limit yourself to only one aspect of modeling.

How can you find out about a local model railroading club? Start by checking with your hobby shop owner. He or she probably belongs to a club or knows of other people who do. There are also listings of local clubs in many model railroading magazines. Lists are also available from the National Model Railroad Association in Chattanooga, Tennessee, or some of the other organizations listed in the next chapter of this book.

Once you have located a club, call a member and find out when the next meeting is scheduled. Even if you're just a beginner, the other club members will be glad to have you join. Every club needs new members!

If there is no club nearby, consider forming one. Put a notice in the school paper or in a local newspaper or post one on a school bulletin board or at a hobby shop. You might try something like this:

TO ALL SERIOUS MODEL RAILROADERS: LET'S BRING OUR HOBBY OUT OF THE BASEMENT. IF YOU WOULD LIKE TO FORM A CLUB TO SHARE IDEAS AND PLAN SHOWS AND OTHER EVENTS, CONTACT (YOUR NAME) AT/IN (YOUR PHONE NUMBER OR HOMEROOM CLASS NUMBER).

Plan on holding the first few meetings at different members' houses to view their setups and plans. See what each of you has in common and how your ideas can help each other's interests grow. Consider developing a set of club rules and goals. The two things your club should insist on is that members be serious about their hobby and that they be willing to share ideas with each other. Beyond that, the rest of the rules are up to the group. For example, you might agree that different members will subscribe to certain magazines or guidebooks. They can share their copies and save money. You also might have different members present workshops on layouts, scenery building, wiring, weathering, or some other techniques. The workshops could be just for club members. Or you might invite outsiders to attend and learn more about the hobby. That would be a good way to recruit new members for the club.

Also take photographs or videos of your club members' setups, particularly those that look realistic. The local or

Clubs offer modelers the chance to be involved with a larger layout than they may be able to build at home.

school newspaper will probably be happy to publish the photographs, and that could help promote the club and the hobby too.

One of the things that makes model railroading special is that there is always something new to learn. And a model railroading club can help make the learning easier and more fun. So don't be shy—share!

FOR MORE INFORMATION

This book is only a starting point. There are many more sources of information you should explore as you learn about model railroading and try your hand at the hobby. Here are some good places to turn for more information:

ASSOCIATIONS & ORGANIZATIONS

National Model Railroad Association
4121 Cromwell Road
Chattanooga, TN 37421
(615) 892-2846
This is the major organization in model railroading, founded in 1935. The association publishes a monthly bulletin and many different guidebooks and lists of standards for the hobby.

Toy Train Collectors Society
109 Howedale Drive
Rochester, NY 14616

Train Collectors Association
P.O. Box 248
Stroudsburg, PA 18360
These two organizations are more for the serious collector than the amateur modeler. The Train Collectors Association also maintains a special museum in Stroudsburg that you may want to visit sometime.

PERIODICALS

Below is a list of magazines that will appeal to those interested in model railroading or, in some cases, in full-size trains. Most issues contain interesting and useful ideas to try out on your own systems, including track layouts or wiring techniques. Most have numerous ads for equipment and a classified section if you're interested in trading, buying, or selling equipment, or in forming a model railroading club.

Classic Toy Trains and Model Railroader
Kalmbach Books
21027 Crossroads Circle
P.O. Box 1612
Waukesha, WI 53187

NMRA Bulletin
National Model Railroad Association
4121 Cromwell Road
Chattanooga, TN 37421

Railroad Model Craftsman and Rail Fan
Carstens Publications, Inc.
P.O. Box 700
Newton, NJ 07860

Railroad Modeler and Rail Classics
Challenge Publications, Inc.
7950 Deering Avenue
Canoga Park, CA 91304

You might also want to obtain catalogs of locomotives, rolling stock, and scenery and ready-to-build kits from Walthers Inc., one of the largest model railroading distributors in the world. The company's address is:

Walthers, Inc.
5601 West Florist Avenue
Milwaukee, WI 53218

BOOKS

A variety of general books on model railroading and those focusing on specific subjects such as layouts and track plans, wiring, and scenery are available from the following publishers. You can find many of the books in your public library or in hobby shops, or you could contact the publishers directly at the addresses listed below:

Atlas Railroad Books
Atlas Tool Co., Inc.
378 Florence Avenue
Hillside, NJ 07205

Carstens Publications, Inc.
P.O. Box 700
Newton, NJ 07860

Greenberg Publishing Co.
7566 Main Street
Sykesville, MD 21784

Kalmbach Books
21027 Crossroads Circle
P.O. Box 1612
Waukesha, WI 53187

Kemtron Corp.
P.O. Box 360
Walnut, CA 91789

Walthers, Inc.
5601 West Florist Avenue
Milwaukee, WI 53218

GLOSSARY

AC (alternating current)—Household current in which the flow of electrons reverses direction in cycles. A power pack or transformer is used in a model train setup to convert alternating current to direct current.

collector—A model railroader whose main interest is owning and displaying model trains rather than building layouts and operating trains on them.

DC (direct current)—Current in which electrons flow in only one direction. Most model train locomotives run on direct current rather than alternating current.

diorama—A miniature scene that consists of three-dimensional (3-D) models or figures placed in front of a scenic backdrop.

gauge—The width of track of a real or model railroad as measured from the inside of one rail head to the inside of the other.

HO scale—A scale of model railroads or equipment which is $1/87$ the size of the original. For example, a 40-foot boxcar would be only $5^1/_2$ inches long in HO scale.

modeler—A model railroader who enjoys creating layouts and scenery and operating trains within a total model environment.

modular model railroading—The creation of a model railroad setup in small, portable segments. Often modules can be linked together to form a large, complete railroad.

N scale—A scale of model railroads and equipment that is $1/160$ the size of the original. For example, a 40-foot boxcar would be only 3 inches long in N scale.

narrow gauge—Railroads that were built with their rails spaced closer together than the government standard of 56½ inches. Narrower track and narrow gauge trains were often used in mountainous areas or other areas where tight turns were necessary.

National Model Railroad Association (NMRA)—The major organization in model railroading. The NMRA produces numerous publications and publishes standards that are followed by most model railroaders.

O scale—A scale of model railroads and equipment that is 1/40 the size of the original. For example, a 40-foot boxcar would be 1 foot long in O scale.

power pack—An electrical device that plugs into a household outlet and converts 110 volt AC current into 12 volt DC power to run a model railroad locomotive. Power packs often contain both DC and AC terminals for powering trains and accessories.

rail joiner—A small, metal, electrically conductive clip used to join two sections of model railroad track.

rolling stock—Freight or passenger cars of a real or model railroad.

scale—The proportion of a miniaturized model to a full-size original train. The most common scales of model trains are HO, N, and O, but there are a total of 17 scales recognized by the NMRA.

standard gauge—Railroads that were built with their rails spaced according to the government standard of 56½ inches.

switch—A portion of railroad track where two lines come together and where trains can change routes. Another word for a switch is a *turnout*.

trestle—A bridge and its supporting structure.

turnout—A portion of track where two diverging lines join. A turnout is also called a *switch*.

weathering—The process by which model railroaders use chalk or paint to make their railroad cars or scenery look older and weather-beaten and thus more realistic.

INDEX

assembly 22, 23, 24
associations 41
auction 11

bodies of water 25, 31, 33
book publishers 43, 44
bridges 25, 33
building the setup 28

caboose 20
clockwork mechanism 9
coal-fired steam locomotive 10
collecting 9, 10, 11
crossings 27
current 23, 29

derailments 23, 27, 28, 29
diesel locomotive 20
diorama 33, 36
displaying 10
dust 22, 23

electric locomotive 20
electrical contact 22
elevated tracks 28
embankments 33

freight trains 15, 16, 20

gauge 6, 15, 16, 17, 18, 20

historical period trains 20
HO scale 16, 17, 18
hobby stores 9, 14, 15, 21, 25, 29, 30, 31, 32

instructions 22

kits 13, 20, 31, 33

laying track 29
liquid latex 32
liquid plastic 33
locomotives 9, 10, 11, 13, 20, 28
loop 29, 30

maintenance equipment 20
model railroading, history and introduction 10,
    11, 13
model railroading clubs 15, 38, 39, 40
modelers 11, 13
modules 36, 37
mountains 25, 31, 32
multiple controls 30

N scale 16, 17, 37
nails 29
narrow gauge 6, 18

National Model Railroad Association (NMRA) 16, 38
needle-nose pliers 22

O scale 16, 18, 37
oiling, avoidance of 22

paint 35
passenger trains 15, 16, 20
periodicals 42
planning layout 25, 26, 27, 28, 29, 30
plaster 32
plywood 16, 23, 28
polystyrene 33
portable setup 14
power pack 22, 23, 24, 25, 29, 30

rail joiners 23
rail ties 29
railroad building, history of 6
research and preparation 14, 15, 16, 17, 18, 20, 21
resin 33
roadbeds 28, 29
rolling stock 17, 18, 20

sandpaper 22, 34
scale 13, 16, 17, 18, 19, 20, 25, 26
scale models 6, 13
scenery 16, 25, 26, 27, 28, 31, 32, 33, 36
short circuit 30
sketch 25, 28
space considerations 14, 16, 17, 27, 33
spray painting 35
standard gauge 18
steam locomotive 20
switches 6, 26, 27

templates, track 25
terminals 22, 23, 29
tools 15, 22, 25
track 6, 11, 22, 23, 26
track plan 25, 28, 33
train set, basic 22, 26
trains 5, 15, 16, 20
trestle 10, 25
tunnels 6, 15, 25, 31, 32, 33
turnouts 27

voltage 23

walls and fences 31
weathering 10, 34, 35
wiring 15, 29, 30
wound spring mechanism 9